Nature Spotter
MINIBEASTS

CATHERINE BRERETON

Illustrated by
KATE McLELLAND

BLOOMSBURY
CHILDREN'S BOOKS
LONDON OXFORD NEW YORK NEW DELHI SYDNEY

BLOOMSBURY CHILDREN'S BOOKS
Bloomsbury Publishing Plc
50 Bedford Square, London WC1B 3DP, UK
Bloomsbury Publishing Ireland Limited
29 Earlsfort Terrace, Dublin 2, D02 AY28, Ireland

BLOOMSBURY, BLOOMSBURY CHILDREN'S BOOKS and the Diana logo
are trademarks of Bloomsbury Publishing Plc

First published in Great Britain 2026 by Bloomsbury Publishing Plc

Text copyright © Bloomsbury, 2026
Illustrations copyright © Kate McLelland, 2026

All rights reserved. No part of this publication may be: i) reproduced or transmitted in any form, electronic or mechanical, including photocopying, recording or by means of any information storage or retrieval system without prior permission in writing from the publishers; or ii) used or reproduced in any way for the training, development or operation of artificial intelligence (AI) technologies, including generative AI technologies. The rights holders expressly reserve this publication from the text and data mining exception as per Article 4(3) of the Digital Single Market Directive (EU) 2019/790

A catalogue record for this book is available from the British Library

ISBN: 978-1-5266-9844-5

2 4 6 8 10 9 7 5 3 1

Text by Catherine Brereton

Printed and bound in China by Toppan Leefung Printing, DongGuan, GuangDong

To find out more about our authors and books visit
www.bloomsbury.com and sign up for our newsletters
For product safety related questions contact productsafety@bloomsbury.com

Published under licence from RSPB Sales Limited to raise awareness of the RSPB (charity registration in England and Wales no. 207076 and Scotland no. SC037654).

For all licensed products sold by Bloomsbury Publishing Limited, Bloomsbury Publishing Limited will donate a minimum of 2% from all sales to RSPB Sales Ltd, which gives all its distributable profits through Gift Aid to the RSPB.

The RSPB is the UK's largest nature conservation charity. With your help, they can protect wild spaces and create a bright future for wildlife.

CONTENTS

LET'S SPOT MINIBEASTS	4
HABITATS	5
WORMS, SLUGS AND SNAILS	6
SPIDERS	10
INSECTS	14
BUTTERFLIES AND MOTHS	38
OTHER MINIBEASTS	44
OUTDOOR ACTIVITIES	46
NATURE SCRAPBOOK	48

LET'S SPOT MINIBEASTS

This book will help you spot and name many of the minibeasts you see around you. There is so much to discover!

How to use your spotting guide

Use the pictures to help you identify the minibeasts you spot. Place the stickers on the matching pages each time you make a discovery.

The fact boxes display handy information. Here is the key:

⌂ tells you where the minibeast lives (habitat)

✎ tells you the size of the minibeast

▦ tells you when you might see the minibeast. If you don't see a calendar, you can spot the minibeast all year round

Minibeast rules

Try and be quiet and still to not startle the minibeasts.

You might be able to handle some minibeasts, but never frighten or hurt them, and always wash your hands after touching them.

Protect habitats. Don't drop litter, or pick or damage plants.

HABITATS

A place where an animal lives is called a habitat. To spot the minibeasts in this book, you will need to visit lots of different habitats.

Gardens and parks
Look out for trees, bushes and flowers – they may be providing a minibeast with food or a home.

Towns and cities – and homes!
Minibeasts can thrive in towns and cities, where you may find bees, flies, spiders, snails, butterflies and moths.

Fields and hedges
Grassy fields and meadows are great places to spot nectar-loving minibeasts like bees and butterflies.

Woods and forests
Woodlands are some of the richest wildlife habitats. Just one tree can support thousands of minibeasts.

Ponds, rivers and lakes
All living things need water – so don't forget to search around ponds, rivers and lakes.

Let's get spotting and sticking!

WORMS, SLUGS AND SNAILS

You'll often find worms, slugs and snails near soil. While worms have completely soft bodies and no legs, slugs and snails have one thick, strong foot which they use to move. Snails also have a hard shell to protect them.

Common earthworm

up to 35 cm

soil everywhere

The common earthworm is a pink-grey worm with a soft body made up of lots of segments. It helps break down rotting leaves and other dead plants.

Common garden slug

The common garden slug is a small black or dark grey slug with tiny gold speckles. It likes to feed on plant roots.

30 mm

gardens, fields

○ common earthworm ○ common garden slug ○ large black slug ○ leopard slug

Large black slug

up to 180 mm

gardens, woods

March – November

The large black slug is usually black, but can also be a brownish-red colour. It has one long foot and moves along on a trail of slime. It munches on rotting plants, fungi and dead animals.

Leopard slug

The leopard slug is a very big slug with spots on its back, just like a leopard. It eats snails, animal poo and sometimes other slugs!

up to 20 cm

gardens, woods

WORMS, SLUGS AND SNAILS

up to 40 mm across (shell)

gardens, farmlands, woods, hedgerows

Garden snail

The garden snail is one of the most well-known creatures you'll see outside. Its shell has dark blotches and yellow zig-zag stripes.

Banded snail

Banded snails have a pale body and a stripy shell that can vary in colour. The stripes follow the shell's spiral pattern. These markings help the snail camouflage in the grass and hide from birds.

up to 25 mm across (shell)

grasslands, woods, gardens

Great pond snail

45–65 mm (shell length)

ponds

The great pond snail has a large, brown, pointed spiral shell and two triangle-shaped tentacles on its head. It eats almost anything in ponds.

Great ramshorn snail

This snail has a reddish-brown shell with a flattened spiral shape that makes it look a bit like the curled horn of a ram (a male sheep). This is where its name comes from!

30 mm across (shell)

ponds, drains

SPIDERS

Spiders are made up of a head, thorax, abdomen and eight legs. They often have lots of eyes. They also have the amazing ability to make silk.

Giant house spider

up to 74 mm (leg span)

indoors

This large spider has a dark hairy body and long legs. It likes to live in people's homes. It can survive for months without eating.

Wolf spider

The wolf spider is a grey-brown colour. Like a wolf, it leaps on its prey. There are 38 species of wolf spider in the UK.

up to 8 mm (body)

gardens, farmlands, woods

March – July

giant house spider · wolf spider · garden spider · cellar spider

Garden spider

The garden spider has a big round body and eight thick hairy legs. It builds a new web daily, in order to catch insects.

up to 18 mm (body)

gardens, meadows, woods, farmlands

June – November

up to 70 mm (leg span)

indoors

Cellar spider

The cellar spider has a small pale body and long, thin legs. If disturbed, it vibrates its web so quickly that its body becomes almost invisible!

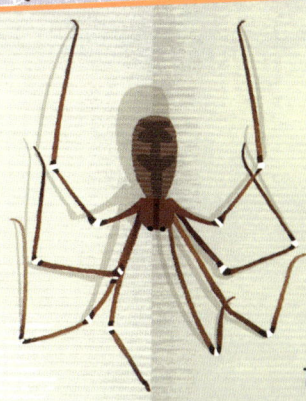

SPIDERS

up to 15 mm (body)

freshwater, wetlands

Water spider

The water spider lives underwater in lakes, ponds and streams. It spins its web between pond plants, where it traps air bubbles from the water's surface. It stays in these bubbles most of the time, only rushing out to catch prey.

Money spider

The money spider has a round, shiny, tiny black body. There are over 250 species of money spider in the UK.

up to 8 mm (body)

gardens, woodlands, parks, fields

June – October

Zebra spider

This spider has black-and-white stripes and two big eyes. It needs good eyesight because it hunts for food, rather than spinning a web.

up to 7 mm (body)

gardens, farmlands

April – October

A zebra spider is a jumping spider. It pounces on its prey using its powerful back legs.

INSECTS

Insects are one of the biggest and most varied groups of animals on the planet. All insects have six legs and antennae or feelers, and are made up of the head, thorax and abdomen.

Emperor dragonfly

Male emperor dragonflies have a long, thick, blue body. Females are green or blue. They both have four see-through wings, and are expert fliers.

78 mm (body)

ponds, lakes, canals, rivers

April – September

The emperor dragonfly is the biggest dragonfly in Britain!

○ emperor dragonfly ○ common field grasshopper ○ common green grasshopper

Common field grasshopper

The common field grasshopper is brown or green with a pinkish patch on its bottom. It makes chirruping sounds by rubbing its back legs against its front wings.

18 – 24 mm (wingspan)

gardens, grasslands, farmlands, moorlands

May – October

Up to 23 mm

grasslands, heathlands, moorlands

April – September

Common green grasshopper

This grasshopper is pale green with brownish sides. Male grasshoppers sing to impress females. Its song can last for more than 20 seconds.

INSECTS

Large red damselfly

The male large red damselfly has red eyes and a long red abdomen with black stripes. The females vary in colour – from mostly red to mostly black.

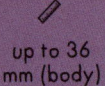
up to 36 mm (body)

wetlands, ponds, wet woodlands, grasslands

March – September

Blue-tailed damselfly

The male blue-tailed damselfly has a brilliant blue segment at the end of its abdomen. Look for it on plants next to canals, lakes, ponds and slow-moving streams.

31 mm (body)

freshwater, wetlands, woodlands, gardens

April – September

- large red damselfly
- blue-tailed damselfly
- emerald damselfly
- common blue damselfly

Emerald damselfly

The emerald damselfly is metallic green with pale blue eyes. Unlike most damselflies, it holds its wings half-open while perching.

38 mm (body)

freshwater, wetlands

May – October

Common blue damselfly

This damselfly is a thin, dainty insect. Males are bright blue and females are bright blue or dull green. You may see a mating pair flying together.

33 mm (body)

ponds, rivers, canals, lakes, woods

April – October

INSECTS

Speckled bush-cricket

The small speckled bush-cricket is bright green, with tiny black speckles and a stripe on its back. It sings by rubbing its wings together.

9 – 18 mm

gardens, grasslands, woods, farmlands

May – November

up to 17 mm

hedgerows, gardens, woods

May – November

Dark bush-cricket

This cricket is a dark reddish-brown colour, with a greenish-yellow belly. It has a big, bulky body. Like a grasshopper, it has long, strong legs for jumping.

speckled bush-cricket | dark bush-cricket | common green shield bug | forest bug

Common green shield bug

Up to 13.5 mm

gardens, parks, farmlands, woods, woodlands

May – November

In the summer, the common green shield bug is a bright green colour. In winter, its front wings turn brown, just like dead leaves!

Forest bug

The forest bug is a brown shield bug with an orange spot in the centre of its shield. It feeds on tree sap, as well as fruits and small insects.

11 – 14 mm

woods, gardens, parks, orchards

June – November

INSECTS

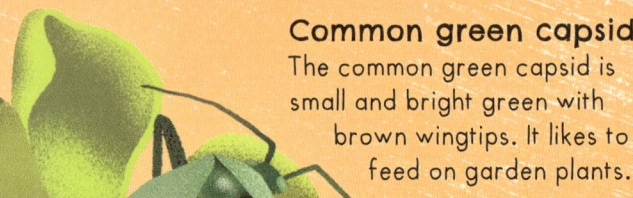

Common green capsid
The common green capsid is small and bright green with brown wingtips. It likes to feed on garden plants.

6.5 mm

gardens, woodlands, grasslands

June – October

up to 2 mm

gardens, woods

March – August

Peach-potato aphid
Peach-potato aphids are bright green, pear-shaped bugs. They spend their lives sucking plant sap, and can cause a lot of damage to garden plants and crops.

Green tiger beetle

The green tiger beetle is bright green with long purple legs and cream spots on its wing cases. Like a tiger, it is a fierce hunter with very powerful jaws.

10 – 11 mm

heathlands, sand dunes, grasslands

April – September

Stag beetle

The stag beetle is the biggest land beetle in Europe. It is a shiny brownish-black colour. The males use their huge jaws to fight one another.

up to 75 mm

woods, gardens, parks, hedgerows

May – August

INSECTS

Common sexton beetle

The common sexton beetle is black with orange or red patches on its wing cases. It does a very important job for the environment – it buries dead animals, like mice.

up to 30 mm

woods, farmlands, grasslands, gardens

April – October

Thick-legged flower beetle

The thick-legged flower beetle is long, shiny and green. The males have funny-looking bulges on their back legs.

up to 11 mm

grasslands, gardens

April – September

common sexton beetle · thick-legged flower beetle · great diving beetle · whirligig beetle

Great diving beetle

This very large beetle is dark brown or black with yellow legs. It injects its prey with a chemical that turns its insides to liquid – which the beetle then sucks up!

up to 30 mm

ponds, slow-moving waters

Whirligig beetle

The whirligig beetle has two pairs of eyes. When it hunts on the water, one pair of eyes looks underwater for prey, while the other pair of eyes looks above the water for predators!

5–7 mm

ponds, lakes, ditches, slow-flowing rivers

INSECTS

up to 6 mm

woodlands, gardens, grasslands, farmlands, coasts

March – October

Two-spot ladybird

The two-spot ladybird is red with one black spot on each wing case. Like most ladybirds, it feeds on aphids.

Seven-spot ladybird

The seven-spot ladybird has three black spots on each wing, with the seventh split between the two. It is loved by gardeners because it eats damaging aphids.

6 – 8 mm

gardens, grasslands, woods, towns, cities, farmlands

March – October

○ two-spot ladybird ○ seven-spot ladybird ○ 14-spot/22-spot ladybird ○ harlequin ladybird

14-spot/22-spot ladybird

The 14-spot and 22-spot ladybird are yellow with black spots. The 14-spot ladybird has rectangular spots. The 22-spot ladybird has round spots which never merge.

3 – 5 mm

grasslands, woodlands, farmlands, gardens

April – August

8 mm

grasslands, farmlands, woodlands, towns, gardens

March – November

Harlequin ladybird

There are many variations of the harlequin ladybird – for example, it can be black with red spots, or red with black spots. It is a non-native species, and was first seen in the UK in 2004.

INSECTS

15 – 25 mm

gardens, woods, hedgerows, grasslands

June – July

Glow-worm

The glow-worm is not a worm, but a beetle. The female has a thick, worm-like body, and glows in the dark!

Glow-worm larvae stab, poison and eat lots and lots of slugs and snails.

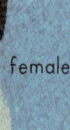
female

glow-worm   cockchafer   bee chafer

Cockchafer

up to 35 mm

woods, gardens

May – July

Cockchafers are large brown beetles. The males have fan-shaped antennae. They fly around in groups on summer nights, making a whirring, buzzing sound.

Bee chafer

The bee chafer is a beetle that looks like a bee. It also buzzes when it flies. This disguise makes predators think it can sting like a bee.

Bee chafers are quite rare in the UK.

up to 10 mm

gardens, grasslands

May – July

INSECTS

Silverfish

The silverfish has shiny silvery scales and a fish-like way of wriggling. It likes to live in damp nooks and crannies in kitchens and bathrooms. It doesn't have wings.

up to 12 mm

towns, gardens

Common earwig

The common earwig is a shiny brown insect with a long body, long antennae and pincers on its back end. It scurries about at night.

up to 18 mm

gardens, parks, woods, grasslands

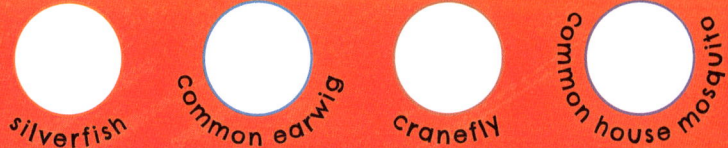

silverfish • common earwig • cranefly • common house mosquito

Cranefly

The cranefly has a thin body and very long, fragile legs. It's also known as a daddy-long-legs. Most adult craneflies do not eat at all.

up to 50 mm (legs)

ponds, lakes, grasslands, gardens

June – September

Common house mosquito

4 – 10mm

freshwater, gardens, towns, woodlands, grasslands

May – August

The common house mosquito is a little fly known for its bite. The female's mouth is a sharp tube, which she pricks animals with before feeding on their blood. Male mosquitoes feed on nectar.

INSECTS

12 – 15 mm

ponds, especially quiet, still ones without fish

April – November

Pond skater

Pond skaters are grey water bugs with long legs. They use their front legs to hold their prey, their middle legs to row or jump, and their back legs to steer. They have waterproof hairs on their feet that help them skate over the surface of the pond.

There are 9 species of pond skater in the UK.

Water scorpion

up to 35 mm

ponds, shallow lakes

The water scorpion is a bug, not a scorpion. It has a long brown body, pincer-like front legs, and a long tube on its bottom that it uses like a snorkel.

Water stick insect

The water stick insect has a thin, stick-like body and a long tail. It grabs its prey with its front legs. It is a relative of the water scorpion.

50 mm

freshwater, wetlands

INSECTS

Marmalade hoverfly

The marmalade hoverfly has a yellow-and-black striped body like a wasp, which tricks predators into thinking it can sting. Hoverflies are some of our most important pollinators.

10 mm

gardens, parks, woods, grasslands

Housefly

The housefly has a brown-and-black stripy body and bright red eyes. There are many different species of housefly – it is one of the most common insects in the world.

7 mm

houses, farms, rubbish dumps

April – October

 marmalade hoverfly  housefly  horse fly  fruit fly

Horse fly

The horse fly is a large brown fly. The females are known for biting farm animals, and sometimes people. They hum loudly before attacking.

10 mm

farmlands, wetlands, woodlands, heathlands,

May – September

Fruit fly

3 mm

gardens, orchards, hedgerows

May – August

The fruit fly is brown with red eyes. You may see one hovering around fruit in your kitchen, sipping on any drops of juice that ooze out.

INSECTS

Bluebottle

14 mm

houses, gardens

April – September

The bluebottle is a big, round fly with a shiny blue-black body and hairy bristles. The female feeds and lays her eggs on rotting meat. The eggs hatch into larvae called maggots.

Greenbottle

The greenbottle is a bright, shiny green fly with big, red eyes. It is smaller than the bluebottle and tends to stay outdoors.

9 mm

gardens, parks, fields

Black garden ant

The black garden ant is a tiny, busy insect with pincer-like jaws. You'll see it scurrying about looking for nectar, soft fruit and other insects to eat.

3 – 5 mm

gardens, parks, farmlands

March – October

Red ant

up to 6 mm

gardens, parks, farmlands, grasslands

The red ant is a red-brown colour with a black abdomen. It feeds on scraps of dead animals and kills other minibeasts with a powerful sting!

INSECTS

Common wasp

The common wasp is a stripy yellow-and-black insect. It lives in a large colony. The queen chews up wood to make paper for building the nest.

 up to 25 mm
 most habitats
 April – October

Hornet

The hornet is about twice the size of a common wasp, with stripes that are brown and yellow rather than black and yellow. It is less aggressive than the common wasp.

 up to 35 mm
 woods, parks, gardens
 May – November

Red-tailed bumblebee

11 – 22 mm

gardens, woods, farmlands, moorlands

March – September

The female red-tailed bumblebee is big and round with a red-orange bottom. The male is smaller, and has yellow bands as well as a red tail. They like to feed on flat-faced flowers such as daisies.

Buff-tailed bumblebee

The buff-tailed bumblebee is big and hairy. While the queen's tail is completely buff (pale brown), worker bees have a white tail with a thin buff stripe.

up to 22 mm

gardens, towns, cities, grasslands, farmlands, hedges

February – September

BUTTERFLIES AND MOTHS

Butterflies and moths have furry bodies, four wings and a long proboscis (a tube they use for sucking up food, like nectar). Butterflies tend to be active in the day, whereas most moths come out at night.

Meadow brown

The meadow brown butterfly is a common, medium-sized butterfly. It is mainly brown with a black eyespot on each forewing.

up to 55 mm (wingspan)

fields, meadows, parks, gardens, woods, hedgerows

June – September

meadow brown  orange-tip  clouded yellow

Orange-tip

The female orange-tip butterfly is white with black wingtips and a black spot on each forewing. It is only the male that has bright orange tips. The male also has a mottled green underwing.

40 – 50 mm (wingspan)

riverbanks, hedgerows, meadows, gardens

April – July

up to 62 mm (wingspan)

many open habitats

May – November

Clouded yellow

The clouded yellow butterfly is large and yellow. It nearly always rests with its wings closed, showing a white-and-silver spot like a number 8 in the middle of its hindwing.

BUTTERFLIES AND MOTHS

Small tortoiseshell

The small tortoiseshell butterfly is actually quite a large butterfly. It is bright orange with black-and-yellow bars and spots.

50 – 56 mm (wingspan)

woods, grasslands, gardens, towns, cities

January – November

Painted lady

50 – 56 mm (wingspan)

most habitats

March – October

The painted lady is a large orange butterfly with black-and-white wingtips and black markings all over its wings. It is a very strong flier, and can travel over 100 miles a day.

small tortoiseshell　painted lady　red admiral　common blue

Red admiral

Up to 72 mm (wingspan)

most habitats

March – November

The red admiral is a large red-and-black butterfly. Look out for one sitting in a sunny place with its wings open – it is trying to warm up before it takes flight!

Common blue

This small butterfly likes warm, grassy places. The male has blue wings, while the female has brown wings.

 male

 female

35 mm (wingspan)

gardens, meadows, woods, coasts

May – October

41

BUTTERFLIES AND MOTHS

Silver Y

This moth is mottled grey and brown with a silver upside-down Y on its forewings. It rests with its wings held back against its body.

up to 42 mm (wingspan)

woodlands, wetlands, gardens, grasslands, farmlands

up to 78 mm (wingspan)

gardens, meadows, riverbanks, sand dunes, woods

July – August

Garden tiger

The garden tiger moth is very colourful, which warns predators that it tastes horrible. It can also make a hissing noise, and ooze a nasty yellow fluid from its head.

○ silver Y   ○ garden tiger   ○ emperor moth   ○ oak eggar

Emperor moth

This is a large moth with brown, gold, grey, cream and orange wings and four bright eyespots. The males have feathery antennae.

up to 80 mm (wingspan)

grasslands, heathlands, moorlands, coasts

March – May

Oak eggar

The oak eggar is brown with a yellow band and a white spot on each forewing. It gets its name because its cocoon is shaped like an acorn from an oak tree.

up to 75 mm (wingspan)

grasslands, moorlands, hedgerows, sand dunes

May – August

OTHER MINIBEASTS

Some minibeasts are not worms, slugs, snails, insects or spiders. Woodlice, for example, are crawling creatures with hard armour plates and seven pairs of legs. They are technically crustaceans.

Common woodlouse

14 mm

gardens, woods, farmlands

The common woodlouse is a shiny grey-black creature with armour plates on its back. It has seven pairs of short legs and lives in cool, damp places.

Woodlice shelter under damp logs and eat the rotting wood they find there.

common woodlouse · white-legged snake millipede · brown centipede

White-legged snake millipede

The white-legged snake millipede has about 100 legs. It comes out at night to feed on dead plants.

up to 30 mm

gardens, woods, farmlands

Brown centipede

The brown centipede is long and reddish-brown. It looks a bit like it has been squashed flat. It has venomous claws on its head.

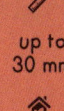

up to 30 mm

woods, grasslands, gardens

OUTDOOR ACTIVITIES

Try these outdoor activities to make wildlife spotting super fun. Reward yourself with a sticker each time you try a new activity!

Go on a woodland bug hunt

Woods are great places to find minibeasts. You can start by getting down on the woodland floor and exploring underneath a log. Make sure to lift it carefully!

Patches of brambles and nettles may have caterpillars munching on their leaves, or bees and butterflies flying around them. Be careful not to get stung!

If you want to get a really close look at a small minibeast, you can use a special bug box. Carefully guide a minibeast into the pot without touching it, and look through the magnifying lid to get a giant's view of the creature.

ADD YOUR STICKER!

MAKE A WORMERY

You will need:
- a two-litre plastic drinks bottle, with the top and bottom cut off by an adult
- a large flowerpot with soil
- card
- soft sand
- crushed chalk
- dead leaves
- ten earthworms, taken carefully from the soil
- a pen

Instructions:
1. Put the earthworms in the flowerpot.
2. Put your cut bottle on top of the soil, and fill it with a 3 cm layer of crushed chalk. Then add a 3 cm layer of sand. Repeat this process until there are multiple 3 cm layers of chalk and sand.
3. Use the pen to mark the levels on the outside of the bottle.
4. Crumble the dead leaves into pieces and sprinkle on top.
5. Wrap the card around and above the bottle to keep light out.
6. Keep damp and leave in a cool place.
7. After a week, remove the card and see what the worms have done. Then release them back into the soil outside.

ADD YOUR STICKER!

NATURE SCRAPBOOK

Your wildlife spotting adventures don't have to stop here. Why don't you create your own minibeast record book? All you need is a notebook, some pencils and an outdoor adventure!

How to make your book

- Draw pictures or take photographs of the interesting minibeasts you spot.
- Create a written record for each minibeast you find, including name, date and time, where you found them and any fun facts.
- Use your 'Just for fun' stickers to decorate your book.

SPOTTING STICKERS

REWARD STICKER

JUST FOR FUN

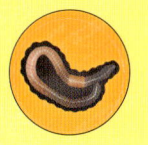 

  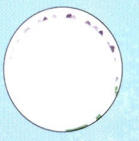